S0-ARK-976

Nature's Cycles
Plants

Dana Meachen Rau

Marshall Cavendish
Benchmark
New York

2

Look at the garden. Plants start small. Then they grow. Soon they flower. They make seeds. Seeds become new plants. This is a plant's *life cycle*.

Some seeds are tiny. Some are big. A coconut is a large seed. An acorn is smaller.

A carrot seed is tiny!

A seed holds a young plant and the food it needs to start growing. A hard cover, called a *seed coat,* keeps the plant safe. A seed starts to grow when the air is warm and the *soil* is moist.

8

When the seed gets wet, the seed coat splits. A *root* comes out the bottom. The root grows down into the ground. It takes in water from the soil.

A *stem* comes out of the top of the seed. It pokes out of the soil. It grows up toward the sun.

Buds form on the stem.
Some buds become leaves.
The leaves use sunlight
to help the plant make
food. This food keeps the
plant growing.

Other buds turn into flowers. Flowers are the parts of plants that make more seeds. Look inside the petals of a flower.

15

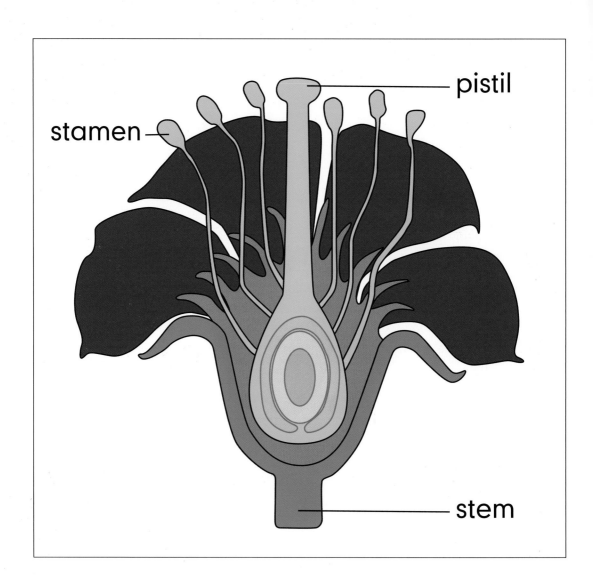

pistil

stamen

stem

Stamens are like sticks poking up from the center. Stamens make *pollen*. The *pistil* is in the center of the flower. It holds tiny eggs.

Pollination happens when pollen travels from the stamen to the pistil. Pollen can travel inside the same flower. It can also travel from one flower to another.

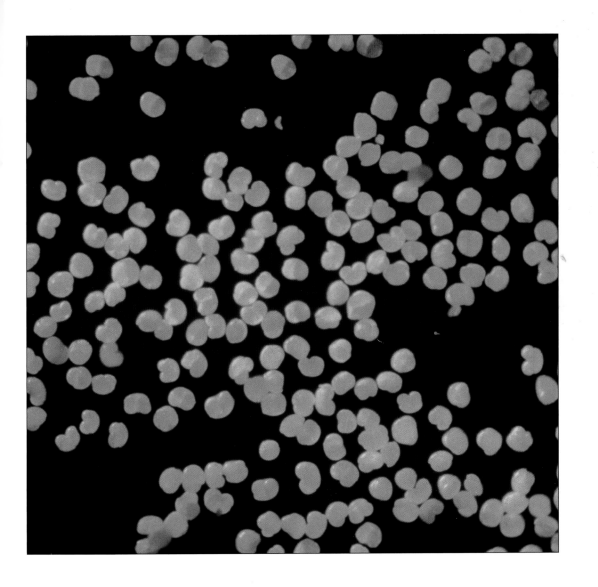

Bees and butterflies help pollinate flowers. Pollen sticks to them when they land on a flower. They bring the pollen to the next flower they visit.

The pollen holds what the egg needs to make seeds. It sends it through a tube into the egg. They come together and make a fruit. The fruit holds seeds inside.

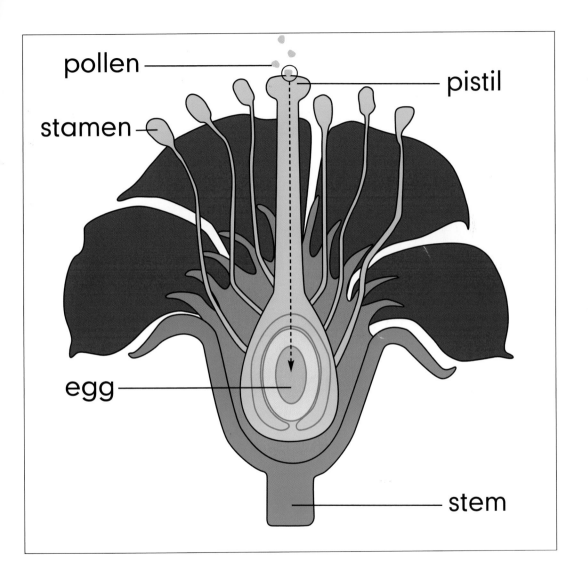

pollen

pistil

stamen

egg

stem

Seeds fall onto the soil. They will grow into new plants.

Some seeds travel. Wind blows seeds through the air. Seeds stick to animals' fur.

Some animals eat seeds.
The seed lands in a new place
when it passes through the
animal's body.

28

A sunflower holds hundreds of seeds. Each seed can make a new plant. One sunflower can make a field of flowers!

Challenge Words

buds—Small bumps on a stem that turn into leaves, flowers, or branches.

life cycle (life SY-kuhl)—The series of things that happen over and over again as a plant grows from a seed, flowers, and then makes more seeds.

pistil (PIS-tuhl)—The part of a flower that holds the eggs and seeds.

pollen—A powdery substance that helps make seeds.

pollination (pol-i-NAY-shun)—When pollen travels from the stamen to the pistil in flowers.

root—The part of a plant that takes in water and food from the soil.

seed coat—The hard cover of a seed.

soil—The earth in which plants grow.

stamens (STAY-mehns)—The parts of the flower that make pollen.

stem—The part of a plant that holds up the leaves and flowers.

Index

Page numbers in **boldface** are illustrations.

The author would like to thank Paula Meachen
for her scientific guidance and expertise in reviewing this book.

With thanks to Nanci Vargus, Ed.D., and Beth Walker Gambro, reading consultants

Marshall Cavendish Benchmark
99 White Plains Road
Tarrytown, New York 10591-9001
www.marshallcavendish.us

Text copyright © 2010 by Marshall Cavendish Corporation

Library of Congress Cataloging-in-Publication Data

Rau, Dana Meachen, 1971–
Plants / by Dana Meachen Rau.
p. cm. — (Bookworms. Nature's cycles)
Includes index.
Summary: "Introduces the idea that many things in the world around us are cyclical in nature and discusses the plant cycle from seed to plant to flower to seed again"—Provided by publisher.
ISBN 978-0-7614-4097-0
1. Plant life cycles—Juvenile literature. 2. Plants—Juvenile literature. I. Title.
QK49.R39 2009
580—dc22
2008042515

Editor: Christina Gardeski
Publisher: Michelle Bisson
Designer: Virginia Pope
Art Director: Anahid Hamparian

Photo Research by Anne Burns Images

Cover Photo by *Getty Images*/Bridget Webber

The photographs in this book are used with permission and through the courtesy of:
Photo Researchers: pp. 1, 15 Mark Burnett; p. 4L F. Stuart Westmorland; p. 4R Michael P. Gadomski; p. 5 Doug Martin; p. 7 John Kaprielian; pp. 8, 11 Mark Boulton; p. 12 Martin Shields; p. 19 James Bell; p. 20 James H. Robinson; p. 24 William Harlow; p. 26 E. R. Degginger; p. 27 Stephen J. Krasemann; p. 28 Holly C. Freeman. *Corbis*: p. 3 Patrick Johns.

Printed in Malaysia
1 3 5 6 4 2